CoolSpeak Publishing Company

The Power of Youth Workbook
By Carlos Ojeda Jr.
Copyright © 2016 CoolSpeak. The Youth Engagement Company
All Rights Reserved.

Graphic and Layout Design: Iske Conradie

Book & Cover design by Carlos Ojeda Jr.

ISBN- 978-0692726822

YOUTH + POWER = CHANGE

By philosophical definition, power is the ability to influence the behavior of others with or without resistance.

By our definition, power is the ability to get things done! The earlier things get done, the better. True power is evident in education, technological advancement, and in revolution, but no more so than in the hands of the youth that make these things happen.

YOUR VOICE IS YOUR POWER

RAISE YOUR HAND

With your voice you can ask questions. Questions give you answers. Answers give you knowledge and knowledge gives you power. The power to change your life, the lives of those you love, your community and this world. Check out this video: https://vimeo.com/137409309 and answer these questions:

? What is your impression of the presentation?

How did it make you feel?

What did it make you think about?

What message did you take from the presentation?

WHAT IS POWER?

By our definition, power is the ability to get things done! The earlier things get done, the better.

But what is power to you? What's your understanding of it and how you can wield it?

 What is Power to you?

Why is it important to have power?

How can power help you change the world?

What are some of the ways you can be a powerful force in the world around you?

 "Power is the ability to get things done!"

THE POWER 5: RULES & CONSEQUENSES

MY FIVE

List five rules you think we should follow:

1.

2.

3.

4.

5.

OUR FIVE

List five rules your group thinks we should follow:

1.

2.

3.

4.

5.

THE FIVE

List the five rules we will follow during this program:

1.

2.

3.

4.

5.

POWER IS WHO YOU ARE...

There is power in who you are. The character you embody, the values you believe in, the behavior you display, and the person people perceive you to be. There is power in just being the person who you are.

THE LOOK & THE FEEL

MIRROR, MIRROR

We are evaluated in the first few seconds based on our appearance, tonality, attitude, body language, language skills, behaviors and more. Those few seconds establish others' opinion of you, whether it is good or bad.

This is why first impressions are very important, because once opinions and decisions are made, at times there's no second chance.

? Who do you mirror?

Who would you like to mirror?

Who would you like to mirror for?

YOU'VE GOT THE LOOK

Take a moment and look through magazines or search the Internet for positive "looks" of individuals you feel are successful and powerful and negative "looks" of individuals that are not successful and powerful. Then describe the "look" you are striving for.

? GOOD "LOOKS"

"Power is the ability to get things done!"

? BAD "LOOKS"

? YOUR LOOK

NOW WORK ON THE FEEL

A wise person once said that when you meet an individual, chances are they will forget your name, what you look like, what you were wearing and what you said, but they will never forget how you make them feel.

GO OUT AND DO SOMETHING NICE FOR SOMEONE...

?

...in your family:

Who:

What:

...in your school:

Who:

What:

...in your community:

Who:

What:

"People will never forget how you make them feel."

ARE YOU ALL IN?

We all have things we want, but how bad do you want it.

 Why do you need to work hard?

Who do you need to work hard for?

What do you need to work hard for?

THE HUSTLE

PAWN SHOP

When you find other people with similar objectives, the job can be done faster and better. But individual and collective effort will determine your overall success. The right people, access to the right resources and the right effort will increase your odds of success.

What did you think of the activity?

How did you feel about the people that showed a lot of effort?

How did you feel about the people that showed little or no effort?

What would you or your team have done different?

Understanding how important effort is, how much effort do you put into the things that are important in your life (school, family, friends etc.)?

What are you going change to make sure you put in the necessary effort to succeed?

What are you going change to make sure you put in the necessary effort to succeed?

THE STRAIGHT SHOT

YOUR WORD IS YOUR BOND

Your intentions could be good, your words could be good, but if you don't do what you say, people will begin to lose trust in you.

CROSS THE LINE

Doing the right thing and being honest, especially without someone watching is a true test of your character. We all place lines for ourselves that we don't cross. Let's see what some of your lines and values are.

? What does being honest mean to you?

How does it feel to do the right, or wrong thing?

How did it feel to see other students disagree with your response?

Why is it important to be honest and do the right thing?

What did you learn from this activity?

LETTER TO SELF

Take a moment to write a letter to your future self. Being honest with yourself about where you are and where you intend to be. Sharing with yourself the goals you wish to accomplish.

"Doing the right thing and being honest."

THE FLASHBACK

WHERE ARE YOU FROM?

Sankofa is an African word that means, "reaching to the past to gain knowledge for the future." It's always important to know our history, our heritage, in order to move forward.

? Where are you from?

WHERE ARE YOU GOING?

Knowing where you are from helps you know where you are going.

? What knowledge can you use from your past, to ensure success in the future?

THE STATEMENT

THIS IS WHO I AM...

Who are you? How do you define yourself? Take 5 minutes and tell us all who you are and hope to be. The direction you are going, what you plan to do, where you plan to go and who you plan to be.

HERE ARE SOME QUESTIONS TO CONSIDER:

? Where are you from and where are you now?

What do you stand for?

What's important to you?

What makes you powerful?

What makes you, you?

 **MY NAME IS ....**
AND I AM THE POWER OF YOUTH!

POWERED ME UP

What Lifted Me Up?

THE POWER METER

POWERED ME DOWN

What Brought Me Down?

POWER IS WHY YU ARE...

There is power in why you are. The reasons of why we do things could be more powerful than the actions themselves. Our "Why" gives us strength to keep going; it tells people the purpose of our actions or goals. People follow you because of why you are doing something, more so than what you are actually doing.

PURPOSE GIVES LIFE MEANING

You know what you want to do, now ask yourself why you want to do it. Asking that simple question will help you arrive to the true reasons for wanting to do exactly what is in your heart and mind. This will help you understand your purpose; help you understand the true meaning of your words and actions. Understanding all of this allows you to plot the way forward to your success.

WHY, WHY, WHY?

 WHY?

WHY?

WHY?

THE MOTIVATION

WHAT MOTIVATES ME?

Motivation pushes us to achieve our goals, even those we think are very difficult. We all have different factors of motivation; why we work so hard and keep going.

What things motivate you?

1.

2.

3.

WHAT ARE MY TRIGGERS?

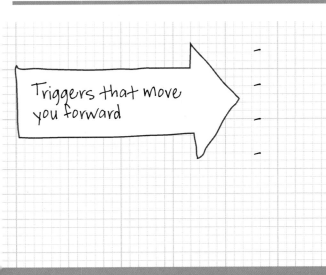

Triggers that move you forward

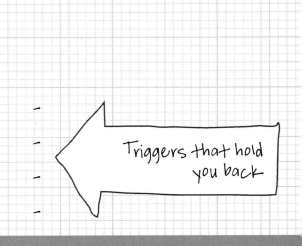

Triggers that hold you back

THE CIRCLES

WHO IS IN YOUR CREW?

? List "mountains" (tasks/goals) that you believe you can't overcome?

Who's in your crew?

Do the people in your circles of influence affect you positively or negatively?

MY CIRCLES OF INFLUENCE

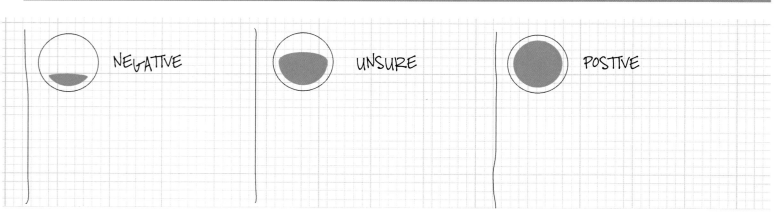

NEGATIVE   UNSURE   POSITIVE

SHIFTING CIRCLES

? What will you do to change the individuals that are in your circle of influence to ensure they impact you in a positive way?

BUILDING YOUR INNER CIRCLE

MENTOR

? Why I want you to be my mentor:

What potential do you see in me?

PEER MENTOR

? Why I want you to be my peer mentor:

What potential do you see in me?

MENTEE

? Why I want to be your mentor:

This is the potential I see in you:

POWER IS WHAT Y⊙U BELIEVE...

There is power in what you believe. For a time it was believed that the earth was flat and this limited how far we would travel and explore our world. This belief prevented us from reaching our full potential. Now, we know better. We've gone from being scared of falling off the edge of the earth to walking on the moon and exploring space. What you believe will dictate how you engage your world and the people in it; it will impact whether you reach your full potential. So, believe in yourself and you will gain power.

THE QUIZ

WHAT YOU BELIEVE

? What do you believe about others? About people that are different than you?

What do you believe about yourself? About people that are similar to you?

Based on your current experience and circumstances, what do you believe about your world? What are your limitations and challenges?

THE MONKEY DID WHAT?

Some times we believe things that simply aren't true. Especially things about what we are capable of. This limits our potential. We'll show you exactly what you are capable of.

1.
2.
3.
4.
5.
6.
7.
8.
9.
10.
11.
12.
13.
14.
15.

? What do you believe now?

THE MOUNTAIN

I CAN'T...

List "mountains" (tasks/goals) that you believe you can't overcome?

1.

2.

3.

I CAN AND THIS IS HOW...

Objective:

How I will accomplish it?

Objective:

How I will accomplish it?

POWER IS WHAT YOU VALUE...

There is power in what you are worth. What's your value? Or should we say, what do you value? What we value can make us wealthy or make us poor. Wealth isn't all about money. There is wealth in our knowledge, wealth in our relationships, wealth in our experience and wealth in all that we value.

THE RICH

WHO IS RICH

? What is rich?

Is rich just about having money?

What does the word rich mean to you?

WHAT DO YOU VALUE

? List the things/people that are valuable to you:
1.
2.
3.
4.
5.
6.
7.
8.
9.
10.

I AM A MILLIONAIRE

? Are you rich? Do you see yourself as a millionaire? Give us three reasons why you are a millionaire, why you are truly rich.

1.

2.

3.

> "Music gives a soul to the universe, wings to the mind, flight to the imagination, and life to everything." ~ Plato

Why Participate in Music?

Playing a musical instrument has been shown to improve students success both in and out of the classroom. Research shows it benefits academic and social growth, improves memory, increases self-esteem and self-discipline, increases grades and test scores and boosts graduation rates.

CONTACT US!

To learn more, contact your student's music teacher or **Bruce Schneider,** *b Instrumental Coordinator*

Bruce Schneider
b Instrumental Coordinator

260.467.7280

bruce.schneider@fwcs.k12.in.us

www.fortwayneschools.org

Wendy Y. Robinson Family and Community Engagement Center
230 E. Douglas Ave.
Fort Wayne, IN 46802

b Instrumental

Making Music Accessible to ALL

FWCS
WE ARE YOUR SCHOOLS

Applying for the program

Pick up an application

See your students music teacher at school for the application or visit fortwayneschools.org/binstrumental

Complete the application

Be sure to complete all sections and sign the application

The Student will Write an Essay or Record a Video

Explain why you are choosing a specific instrument, how you will take care of it, and how you will practice the new instrument.

Turn in the Applicaiton and Essay or Video

Complete and turn in the instrument loan agreement to the music teacher

To apply, visit
fwcs.info/binstrumentalapp

BENEFITS

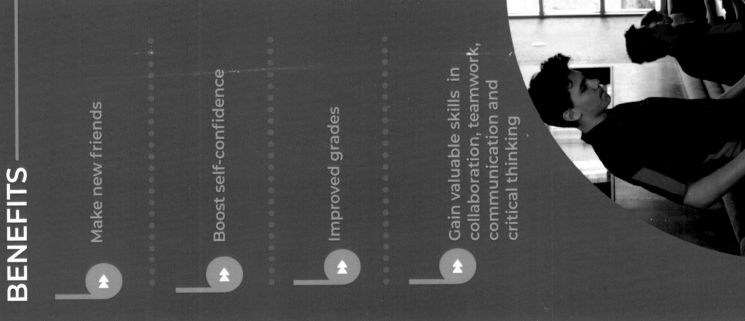

- Make new friends
- Boost self-confidence
- Improved grades
- Gain valuable skills in collaboration, teamwork, communication and critical thinking

What is b Instrumental?

The b Instrumental program provides new or slightly used band and string instruments to Fort Wayne Community School students beginning in grade 7 to use through high school.

Instruments are loaned at no cost to the student or their families thanks to the efforts of the FWCS Foundation and generous gifts from area donors.

b Instrumental also provides free summer music camps and free small group and individual lessons with a teacher that specializes on the student's musical instrument.

POWERED ME UP

What Lifted Me Up?

THE POWER METER

POWERED ME DOWN

What Brought Me Down?

POWER IS WHAT YOU KNOW...

Knowledge is Power. Nothing in this world can be done without it. You can't build, create, develop, or do unless you first know how to do those things. Knowledge is the key to success; with it you can achieve any goal, overcome any obstacle, and arrive at any destination.

THE GAME

WHAT DO YOU KNOW?

If knowledge is power, then you have access to unlimited power. You are more connected to information that any generation before you. You literally have the answer to just about any question at your fingertips. You have power, so let's learn how to use it.

I DON'T KNOW

The words "I don't know," should not exist in your vocabulary. It should never be, "I don't know," it should be, "I'll find out." It should never be, "I can't," it should be, "I'll figure it out."

?

1.

2.

3.

4.

5.

THE SOURCES

WHO'S YOUR HOOK UP?

We all have sources of information. Where do you get most of your information? Who or what is your information hook-up? List your information sources, then brainstorm some new ones.

1.
2.
3.
4.
5.
6.
7.
8.
9.
10.

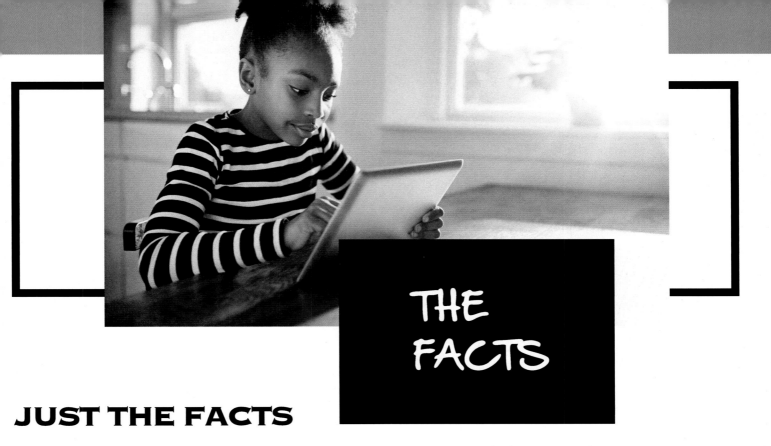

THE FACTS

JUST THE FACTS

Pick a topic (science, history, math, etc.) Make sure the topic is something you are interested in. Challenge yourself to learn one new fact about the topic every day for thirty (30) days. Knowledge is Power.

1.
2.
3.
4.
5.
6.
7.
8.
9.
10.
11.
12.
13.
14.
15.

16.
17.
18.
19.
20.
21.
22.
23.
24.
25.
26.
27.
28.
29.
30.

WHY DO YOU WANT TO KNOW THE FACTS?

? Why is it important to the know the facts? Why do you want to know the odds for and against you? How can it motivate you?

WHAT ARE THE ODDS?

? What are the odds against you? What are the facts?

HOW WILL YOU BEAT THEM?

? What can/will you do to beat those odds and use them for motivation?

POWER IS WHO Y(O)U KNOW

There is power in who you know. We all stand on the shoulders of people that came before us, that help us and are the reason we are who and where we are. No one succeeds alone. In order to succeed, you have to know people, who know people, who know people, who know people, who know people, who know people. There more people you know, the more power you have access to.

"No one is an island. We need each other to succeed."

YOU + HIM + HER + THEM = SUCCESS

Your power is the sum of your power and the power of all the people you know and know you. That is the power of relationship and the reason you should always strive to make new meaningful connections.

MAKE A STATEMENT

No one is an island. We need each other to succeed.

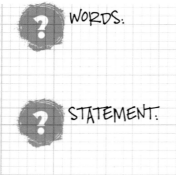

WORDS:

STATEMENT:

THE ELEVATOR PITCH

KNOW PEOPLE WHO KNOW PEOPLE

? Who do you know that can help you or knows someone that can help you? People in your family, at your school, in your community that you can network with.

I'M THE BOMB

? Your elevator pitch should consist of who you are, where you are from, what you do or want to do and why you are the bomb!

THE SHAKE, TAKE & FOLLOW UP

HAND SHAKING 101

? 65% of people don't know how to shake hands properly. Yeah, we are talking about you. Here are some tips on how to give a good handshake.

WHAT'S YOUR NAME & NUMBER

? List the names and email of adults who you just met that can be of help to you.

1. NAME: _____   EMAIL: _____

2. NAME: _____   EMAIL: _____

3. NAME: _____   EMAIL: _____

4. NAME: _____   EMAIL: _____

5. NAME: _____   EMAIL: _____

POWERED ME UP

What Lifted Me Up?

THE POWER METER

POWERED ME DOWN

What Brought Me Down?

POWER IS WHAT YOU SAY...

Words are powerful. Our words can just as easily put a smile or frown on someone's face. Our words can build or destroy, they can heal or wound, they can help us rise or fall. Words can inspire us to find the best within ourselves or be used as weapons of destruction to hold us back. There is power in what you say, so choose your words wisely.

THE WORDS

A PICTURE PAINTS 1000 WORDS...

? But what can six words say about you? Words matter. They are important and they can be deeply meaningful. Come up with a six word statement that defines you, that describes who you are and want to be. For example, mine would be: 'Passionate, creative force for positive change.' Choose your words wisely. Then, write it down, share with your friends and family, post it on your social media, and let everyone know your words.

THE CONVERSATION

WHAT DID YOU SAY?

Words are powerful; and the words you choose to use to express your thoughts and emotions even more so. Learning how to express ourselves can help us communicate and collaborate with others.

? How can words get you in trouble?

How can you use your words to build people up?

How can you avoid miscommunications?

WHAT I'M TRYING TO SAY

? Think about a time where a miscommunication led to an argument or hurting someone's feelings. Now, knowing what you now know about communication, how would restate your thought and/or emotions.

POWER IS HOW YOU USE IT...

Once you have power, you must transform it into influence. How do you use power can determine the outcome of your efforts. Power can be used to oppress others, but power can also be used to serve others. Power can be used to instill justice, or can be used to instill corruption. Power can be used for good, or for evil.

USE IT OR LOSE IT

POWER IS ABOUT SERVICE

Influential people have power, but there are powerful people that have no influence. In order to transform power into influence, you must use your power to help others. A leader's role is to serve. In order to cultivate power you must use it to serve others, serve a greater cause. Do this, and your power will grow.

I WILL USE MY POWER TO...

? What will you use your powers to do?

MY POWER PLAN

Remember Youth + Power = Change. Your voice is your power and you can use it to change your world. It all begins with you. Learn about yourself, about your power, and commit to change your life.

I am: ....
This is my statement: ....
Why i am: ....
What motivates me: ....
When i need to get inspired i will: ....
These are the people in my inner circle: ....
I believe ....
These are the mountains i will climb ....
I'm rich because ....
These are my sources of information ....
This is me in 6 ....
I'm the bomb because ....
With my power i will ....

MY NAME IS ....
AND I AM THE POWER OF YOUTH!

THE SOURCES

KNOWHOW2GO TO COLLEGE

In order to turn these students' college dreams into action-oriented goals, the KnowHow2GO site was launched. It is a multimedia effort that includes television, radio and outdoor public service advertisements (PSAs) that encourage 8th through 10th graders to prepare for college using four simple steps:

Be a pain: Let everyone know that you're going to college and need their help.

Push yourself: Working a little harder today will make getting into college even easier.

Find the right: Find out what kind of school is the best match for you and your career goals.

Put your hands on some cash: If you think you can't afford college, think again. There's lots of aid out there.

Visit knowhow2go.org

NUMBER2.COM

Number2.com is the only website that offers students access to comprehensive free online test preparation courses for the SAT, ACT, and GRE. Students gain access to a customized course that includes user-friendly tutorials, practice sessions that dynamically adapt to each student's ability level, a vocabulary builder, and more.

The site was created and launched by two graduate students studying for their PhDs at Harvard University.

Number2.com is the only website that offers students access to comprehensive free online test preparation courses for the SAT, ACT, and GRE. Students gain access to a customized course that includes user-friendly tutorials, practice sessions that dynamically adapt to each student's ability level, a vocabulary builder, and more.

The site was created and launched by two graduate students studying for their PhDs at Harvard University.

Since 2000, over 2 million students have enrolled in Number2.com's online courses, and the web site now receives over 50 million hits per month.

SCHOLARSHIPS.COM

Since our founding in 1999, Scholarships.com has had one goal: to help students find the money they need to get a college education.

Over the last several years, we've become the largest free and independent college scholarship search and financial aid information resource on the Internet, and have been recognized by high schools, colleges, and universities nationwide.

As a leading scholarship search service and financial aid information resource, Scholarships.com plays a primary role in helping students make the decisions that shape their lives. Our regularly updated proprietary database allows students to search 2.7 million college scholarships and grants worth over $19 billion and quickly arrive at a list of awards for which they qualify.

DOSOMETHING.ORG

DoSomething.org is one of the largest organizations in the US that helps young people rock causes they care about.

A driving force in creating a culture of volunteerism, DoSomething.org is on track to activate two million young people in 2011.

By leveraging the web, television, mobile, and pop culture,

DoSomething.org inspires, empowers and celebrates a generation of doers: teenagers who recognize the need to do something, believe in their ability to get it done, and then take action.

CAREERONESTOP

CareerOneStop is your source for employment information and inspiration. It is the place to manage your career and your pathway to career success. It provides the tools to help job seekers, students, businesses and career professionals find their way to success. It is sponsored by the U.S. Department of Labor.

Visit careeronestop.org

COLLEGEWEEKLIVE

Get college application tips and advice online at CollegeWeekLive, the world's largest college fair. CollegeWeekLive revolutionizes college admissions, making the process easier by saving you time. CollegeWeekLive connects colleges with students, parents, counselors live online.

Join hundreds of colleges and universities from around the world and tens of thousands of high-school students.

Watch college application and admissions experts speak on topics such as how to prepare for the SAT, how to write a winning application essay or how to pay for college. Video chat with college students to learn what campus life is really like.

Visit collegeweeklive.com

MARCH2SUCCESS

How well young men and women do on standardize tests can have a great impact on their future. March2Success was developed as a free, no obligation tool to help anyone improve their test scores in the areas of English, Math and Sciences.

The site provides materials needed to help improve scores on the SAT, ACT and ASVAB.

Our selection of content includes course material from middle and high school level lessons, SAT and ACT practice tests, a SAT/ACT preparation game and vocabulary and math flash cards.

Visit march2success.com

FEDERAL STUDENT AID

Federal Student Aid, an office of the U.S. Department of Education, ensures that all eligible individuals can benefit from federally funded financial assistance for education beyond high school.

We consistently champion the promise of postsecondary education to all Americans —and its value to our society.

Federal Student Aid plays a central and essential role in supporting postsecondary education by providing money for college to eligible students and families. We partner with postsecondary schools, financial institutions and others to deliver services that help students and families who are paying for college.

Visit studentaid.ed.gov

THE RAPID E-LEARNING BLOG

Written and maintained by Tim Kuhlmann, this particular blog offers free tips and advice for new college students. Geared more toward online learning (hence the name), traditional students can also find valuable info.

Visit blogs.articulate.com/rapid-elearning/

EDUCATION QUEST

Designed to provide a solid foundation of support for

college bound high school students, Education Quest offers insight, rich resources, and powerful tools to empower and educate students on what to expect and how to position themselves best for a successful application process and college career.

Visit educationquest.org

STUDY GUIDE ZONE

The site may not be the most updated you'll find in the world of educational resources, but it offers some great, free resources to help students improve their scores on a host of standardized tests, including SAT, ACT, and GED. Great for college-bound students.

Visit studyguidezone.com

GO COLLEGE NOW

A wealth of valuable resources for both students and parents, Go College Now provides info on the best steps to take to get into college, free study resources for standardized tests, and mentorship and funding sources to help pay for it.

Visit gocollegenow.org/for-students-and-parents

COLLEGE GREENLIGHT.

The main listed mission for this site is to "connect first generation and underrepresented students to caring colleges, generous scholarships, and life-changing counselors and mentors." This can be a valuable resources for those students who need it.

Visit collegegreenlight.com

"No one is an island.
We need each other
to succeed."

"Knowledge is power."

"Doing the right thing and being honest."

NOTES

"Power is the ability to get things done!"

"People will never forget how you make them feel."

WHAT'S YOUR NAME & NUMBER

Now it's time work the room and own the room. Network with as many people as possible and get their information.

So you get to know people, who know people, who know people.

NAME: _____   EMAIL: _____

NAME: _____   EMAIL: _____

NAME: _____   EMAIL: _____

NAME: _____   EMAIL: _____

NAME: _____   EMAIL: _____

NAME: _____   EMAIL: _____

NAME: _____   EMAIL: _____

NAME: _____   EMAIL: _____

NAME: _____   EMAIL: _____

NAME: _____   EMAIL: _____

NAME: _____   EMAIL: _____

NAME: _____   EMAIL: _____

NAME: _____   EMAIL: _____

NAME: _____   EMAIL: _____

NAME: _____   EMAIL: _____

NAME: _____   EMAIL: _____

NAME: _____	EMAIL: _____
NAME: _____	EMAIL: _____
NAME: _____	EMAIL: _____
NAME: _____	EMAIL: _____
NAME: _____	EMAIL: _____
NAME: _____	EMAIL: _____
NAME: _____	EMAIL: _____
NAME: _____	EMAIL: _____
NAME: _____	EMAIL: _____
NAME: _____	EMAIL: _____
NAME: _____	EMAIL: _____
NAME: _____	EMAIL: _____
NAME: _____	EMAIL: _____
NAME: _____	EMAIL: _____
NAME: _____	EMAIL: _____
NAME: _____	EMAIL: _____
NAME: _____	EMAIL: _____
NAME: _____	EMAIL: _____
NAME: _____	EMAIL: _____
NAME: _____	EMAIL: _____
NAME: _____	EMAIL: _____
NAME: _____	EMAIL: _____

Made in the USA
Monee, IL
16 August 2022

10961828R00036